Why do We do That?

Commentary on Lawyers

And

The Law

Roberta M. Gubbins

Why do We do That?

Dedicated to Melissa Lucken

Daughter, Professor of Writing and Mentor

Thanks

Published by: Create Space
Cover design by: Darlene Hawver
Visit the author website: http://RobertaMGubbins.com
ISBN: 978-1501092619

Introduction

During my years practicing law, I observed lawyers interact with clients, judges, friends, family and acquaintances. To the casual observer, lawyers' behaviors as they go about their tasks can seem irrational or strange. Even to my family, who knew me well, my behavior, and that of my colleagues was said to be, well, slightly crazy.

It is sometimes hard to understand what makes your lawyer spouse, daughter, son, or friend tick. Why do they keep asking questions until you have no answers and you want to run from the room?

All is revealed in this book, "Why do we do That? Commentary on Lawyers and the Law," a collection of essays written by a lawyer for lawyers and their friends revealing the mysteries of the legal world and the lawyers that inhabit it.

Some are humorous, some serious, and some poignant, but all are meant to engage, entertain and inform so that those who live with and love lawyers and the lawyers themselves, can accept and appreciate their talents.

The law created by lawyers also comes under the microscope. Discover how the law protected two amateur lawyer/writer builders in their efforts to build a chicken coop. Learn why the law is not boring and how a contract for marriage was created in the midst of a football game. I hope reading the essays will bring insight into the world of law and the lawyers who occupy that world.

About the Author

Roberta M. Gubbins is a lawyer who writes. After practicing law for a number of years, she traded her briefcase for a laptop and took up the world of letters. Now she helps lawyers and law firms with their marketing writing needs, ghostwriting blog posts, newsletter articles, biographies, case studies, or ... Always writing with the reader in mind, she translates legalese into plain English, creating informative and interesting articles that future and existing clients can understand and trust.

She is also the editor of Briefs, Ingham County Bar Association e-newsletter and The Mentor, e-newsletter of the State Bar of Michigan Master Lawyers Section.

Her e-book, "Why do We do That? Commentary on Lawyers and the Law," a collection of essays, is now available on Amazon and other e-reader publishers. Using a pen name, Alexandra Hawthorne, she writes cozy mysteries featuring lawyers with extra-human powers and is completing a memoir of her year in Eastern Europe.

Roberta lives in Mason, Michigan with two aloof cats, one Bichon with an attitude problem, assorted fish and a treading water mortgage. She can be reached at roberta@robertamgubbins.com

Table of Contents

The Lawyer in Life

We Need Robes
Bar Card, Bar Code, Bar What?
The Legal Alphabet
Lawyerspeak
The Lawyer Parent
National Lawyer Day
What to Do If…

The Lawyer In Court

Waiting 101
Fun Time at Ye Olde Courthouse
Black's Law Meets Shakespeare
Voir Dire Made Easy
A Lagniappe—Something Extra
Artists and Lawyers Connect the Dots
Techno-Trial in a Techno-Court
The Law of Change
Drive-Through Sentencing
Juvenile Courts: Then and Now

The Lawyer In Society

The Law is Not Boring
The Sun, a Game and a Contract
On Chicken Coops and the Law
The Law and…
Dumb Laws, Wise Laws
Y2K? The Law is Ready
My Summer Vacation or the FBI vs. the ATF
The Pet Who Broke the Rules

Why do We do That?

The Lawyer in Life

We Need Robes

Mention of the English legal system calls to mind barristers in black robes and white wigs speaking in Shakespearean tones before a jury. The public, and to some extent we members of the American Bar, may view barristers as archaic. While some are impressed with the barrister's sense of presence, an understanding of how they work may well cause us to pause and consider this Elizabethan system in a new light. We might envy them their wigs and robes.

The English bar is divided into two distinct groups of attorneys—solicitors and barristers. The barrister's roles are distinguished primarily by two rules. First, the barrister's clients can only come to them via a solicitor and second, generally, only barristers can argue cases before the court.

Let us consider the first rule. How do barristers get clients?

In order to answer that question, one must understand how barristers are organized.

Barristers cannot form partnerships; thus, they have offices in "chambers" or suites of offices. Chambers accommodate anywhere from seven to fifteen barristers. One barrister acts as Head of Chambers or CEO. However, each barrister remains an independent attorney who cannot share fees. The barrister must rely on clients sent by solicitors for work.

Each set of chambers has a clerk (pronounced "clark") whose sole function is to sell the services of the barristers. This clerk does the marketing with the solicitors to bring in the business. He receives five to ten percent of the chamber's gross income as salary. Thus it is in the clerk's best interests to get as much business as possible for the chamber's stable of barristers.

This means, of course, that the barristers do not have to market themselves. No rubber chicken meals, no sitting on boards, no expensive ads in the yellow pages or hours spent on the social media. The clerk does all the work bringing in the solicitors who in turn bring in the clients.

The second rule states that only barristers can argue cases in the higher courts. A solicitor can appear in magistrate's court, but must hire a barrister for his client for other matters that go to trial. It is a rule of etiquette that a barrister cannot appear in court alone and deal with the client himself. The solicitor who hired him must accompany him. The solicitor listens to the client and explains what is happening and why. So, not only do barristers not have to market themselves, they also do not have to talk to clients.

Now, what about files? Do barristers have bulging file cabinets? Are their files stacked on the floor, the desk or cabinet tops awaiting various degrees of attention? No. No files. The solicitors hold the files. The means of communication between the solicitor and the barrister is the 'Brief.'

The brief in the English system is a document telling the barrister what the solicitor wants done. It gives barristers all the information they need to do the job. It appears magically in the barrister's chambers and is tied with a pink ribbon. It is given to the barrister selected by the all-powerful clerk. When the work is done, the brief is returned to the solicitor.

Think about this: barristers do not have to market themselves, do not have to talk to clients and have no files. This is sounding better.

And, lastly, barristers do not negotiate fees. The senior clerk of chambers performs that task.

The clerk will attempt to get as much as possible for the chamber's barristers because— remember—the fee directly affects the clerk's income. The clerk will over-book the barristers keeping them running from court to court. As barristers by custom may not turn down cases, it is possible for the clerk to keep his barristers very busy.

And, in case you were wondering, barristers make decent money. Barristers who become Queen's Counsel (QC) or 'take silk' (so-called because the QC wears a silk robe) generally earn the most. Any barrister can apply for this lofty status after fifteen or twenty years of practice.

The process of selection is secretive. Taking silk brings increased status, higher fees, and the chance to get rid of all paperwork. That's because a junior barrister who totes all the files, takes notes, gets tea, and assists with the case accompanies the QC.

Why do We do That?

Let's review. The barristers do not market themselves. They do not talk to clients. They have no files. They do not negotiate fees. They wear robes and wigs that automatically give them an aura and cover up any spills that occurred during lunch. The wigs are a bit inconvenient as they are made of horsehair, are warm and do tend to give one "wig head." And the robes need to be carried from court to court. But even so, reflect and consider all the advantages of being a barrister. Maybe the time has come for us to lobby for wearing robes like our English counterparts.

Why do We do That?

Bar Card, Bar Code, Bar What?

Did you ever consider the etymology of the word "Bar"? Those of us in the legal profession often use the word—sometimes with a trace of concern, as in " Where did I put that bar card?" Sometimes with authority, as in "The case at bar…" And sometimes (like other mortals) with relief at the end of a long day, as in "Where is the 'coffee' bar?"

There are three pages of definitions of the word "bar" in the Oxford English Dictionary. It is a word of many meanings. Generally, a bar is a piece of any material long in proportion to its thickness or width. A bar has been used to bar entrance to a city. A bar made of wood or iron has been thrown in sporting events. A bar of chocolate may taste very good while a bar of gold would buy many bars of chocolate. Eating all those bars of chocolate could force one to exercise using the barre for balance.

The bar of Michelangelo is the prominence of the frontal bone at the base of the forehead, a characteristic of the heads of his statues. Horses have five bars—one in their mouths where the bar of the bit is inserted, and one on each of their hooves. Bar sinister is the heraldic sign of illegitimacy found on a shield. In an inn or other place of refreshment, a bar is a counter over which food and drink is served to the customers. There are bars of music, bar-bells, bar staff, sand bars, bar boats that carry goods across sand bars and bar boys who guide the bar boats and bar-tailed Godwits who winter in England.

With all those meanings, how did the word come to be identified with the courts and lawyers? We must harken back to fourteenth-century England. Around about that time, barristers organized themselves into Inns of Court. The purpose of the Inns was both social and educational. The bar at the Inns was a barrier or partition that separated the seats of the "benchers" or "readers," AKA students, from the rest of the hall. Once the students had achieved a certain standing, they were summoned from the body of the hall to take part in exercises. Thus they were "called to the bar." "To cast over the bar" was to deprive one of the status of a barrister or to disbar. In time, the entire body of lawyers was called The Bar.

Why do We do That?

The American version of the age-old process is the bar examination that one must pass in order to be "called to the bar." Upon payment of a fee, one gets a bar card. Its only function is to identify the person as a member of The Bar. Remember—we don't have robes to identify us. So if challenged, we can present that little card to prove that we are who we say we are.

There is usually a bar in the courtroom. The bar or partition separates the general public from the space occupied by judges, counsel, jury and others concerned with the matter before the court. We use the term 'the case at bar' to describe the matter before the court.

In British courts, prisoners stand at a barrier or wooden rail, which marks off the judge's space during their arraignment, trials, and sentencing—thus the expression "prisoner at the bar." Those selfsame prisoners can find themselves "behind bars."

The term "bar" has legal significance. A plea at bar was a special pleading constituting an answer to an action that barred or prevented further action by the plaintiff. Bar can mean to defeat, annul or cut off as in "in bar of dower." Under certain circumstances, a judgment rendered in a case is a bar to further action in the state in which it was rendered. In the law of contracts, it is an impediment, obstacle or preventive barrier, as in the "bar" of the statute of limitations.

All these meanings for one three-letter word. There may be even more uses for that little word. So, the next time you as a member of the bar spend a day at the bar arguing the case at bar with fellow bar members, thinking about the bar of gold you will earn doing all that bar work, you might remember some of those meanings or think up some of your own.

The Legal Alphabet

ORDER

At a session of the court held in Ann Arbor, Michigan on January 1, 2001

Pres. Hon. I. M. Judge

It having been observed that the legal community does not have a Legal alphabet by which to organize its affairs; that as a result its files are hopelessly out of order and the court being fully advised in the premises,

IT IS HEREBY ORDERED:

A is for ambactus, a messenger sound
  B is for ballot, a vote going round
C is for carena, which means forty days
  D is for defendant, a client who pays

E is for ejusdem generis, meaning of the same class
  F is for flight, don't run out of gas
G is for generic, any old thing
  H is for hearsay, a song one can't sing

AS THERE ARE MORE LETTERS TO BE DEFINED:

IT IS FURTHER ORDERED:

I is for immunity, a right of exemption
  J is for justice, a hope for redemption
K is for kidnap, meaning to carry away
  L is for licensee, one who is invited to stay

13

Why do We do That?

M is for mandamus, an extraordinary writ
  N is for nullity, an act that doesn't fit
O is for oath, an affirmation of truth
  P is for peeress, a lady of couth

AND, OF COURSE, WE CAN NOT FORGET THE REST SO:

IT IS FURTHER ORDERED:

Q is for quid pro quo, which means consideration
  R is for reasonable doubt, which requires concentration
S is for seriatim, meaning one by one
  T is for trial, your day in the sun

U is for ultra vires, in excess of powers
  V is for verdict, you win, you get flowers
W is for wrongdoer, who runs from the rangers
  X is for xenodochium, an inn for strangers

AND NOW THE BEST:

IT IS FINALLY ORDERED:

Y is for yacht, which carries you away AND
  Z is for zythum, the last drink of the day.

Hon. I. M. Judge Circuit Court Judge

Lawyerspeak

While talking to writer-daughter and gazing out the window one early spring day, I said, "Honey, it appears to me that the tree outside my window may have leaf-like buds on it."

"What kind of statement is that?" asks writer-daughter. "Lawyerspeak?"

That is exactly what it was. Lawyerspeak. By training or by inclination, lawyers speak a language that renders us incapable of making an unequivocal statement. We talk in circles, always leaving an escape route. Our escape route is a way to get out of the words we have just spoken.

How do we escape? We cast our words out into the cosmos to see what will come back. We listen to the words thrown our way to see how we can challenge them. Like a tennis match, our words go back and forth until one side or the other scores a hit.

Our writings also suffer from Lawyerspeak. Professors and other experts advise us to avoid certain words in an effort to make ourselves clear. But even these experts cannot be decisive.

They tell us to "almost never" use the now considered archaic words: hereinafter, to wit, foregoing, wherein, and now comes. We are told by these same experts that we should not use redundant words such as cease and desist, attorney and counselor, stipulate and agree, part and parcel, or made and entered into. Words that we enjoy using and that we lawyers understand. These words are part of us.

We are told to be precise and follow the rules of English composition. We must be clear. But how can we be clear when using the words caveat emptor, nunc pro tunc, quantum meruit or ejusdem generis? Would the statement, "The maxim ejusdem generis is only an illustration of the broader maxim noscitur a sociis" sound as impressive or be as precise if stated: "The maxim of the same class is only an illustration of the broader maxim known by its associates?" The original (used by the Federal Court in State v Western Union) means something to lawyers. The translation into English from the Latin does not carry the same clear meaning.

Lawyers write statutes for other lawyers. They contain the most confusing of all legal language. Open any volume of Michigan Compiled Laws and find redundancies as found in the statute giving villages the power to "restrain and prevent vice and immorality" or to "prohibit and suppress disorderly and gaming houses." Why not simply say the power to "restrain vice" or to "prohibit gaming houses?" Would those words be as impressive? Would they roll off the tongue as forcefully? Would the village believe it had real power? I think not. The statement to "restrain and prevent vice and immorality" somehow has more power than the statement to "restrain vice" alone.

The profession has given up some language. One rarely hears "May it please the court" in this modern world. That expression carries with it the aura of the past. When the expression is used, the courtroom seems to slow down. Some might believe that important words are about to be spoken. Others would think that the attorney is old-fashioned. For whatever reason those words are not used.

Every profession has its own language. Law is no exception. We lawyers are being told that we should give up some of our language. Perhaps we should. Maybe we should say, "The tree has buds." But what if they were not really buds but some other growth? The statement "The tree has buds" has no escape route. We attorneys will always have an escape route. Or maybe the statement should be, "It appears to me that we attorneys will usually, or at least sometimes, want escape routes."

The Lawyer Parent

Ask children who have lawyers for parents and they will tell you said parents are not only a source of embarrassment but can be real drags. As we celebrated Mother's day last month and Father's day this month, it may be time to see ourselves through our children's eyes. The trouble for the child undoubtedly begins before birth.

The gynecologist becomes aware that one of the child's parents is a lawyer. The method of questioning alerts the doctor that you want detailed, soundly reasoned information. Little Jane or Jack is also listening and the discomfiture caused by the lawyer parent is beginning.

Being born doesn't help. Now the scrutiny becomes more intense. Every diaper change is preceded by discussion regarding method, frequency, and type of diaper. More dialogue about the sleep position, the type of food, proper attire perhaps some research is needed before a decision can be made.

"Do the job," the by-now-uncomfortable child thinks. "Is it going to be this way all my life?"

It is time for pre-school. The child is excited about being with his peers. The search for the proper pre-school was long, intense with many high-level parental conferences. Finally, a decision is made and the child is off to school. One day the children are talking about their parents.

"My Mom/Dad is a lawyer," says your child proudly. "What's a lawyer do?" asks Andrea.

"Reads stuff and talks," says your child.

"Is that all?" asks Ed. "My Dad drives a trash truck." "Now that's really cool," says Andrea.

Your child comes home and asks, "Why don't you drive a truck?"

Move on to elementary school. Little Jack, now in second grade, has become resigned to the dullness of your occupation. Career Day is coming up. He comes home with a note from the teacher asking for parents to come in to talk to the class.

Why do We do That?

"You don't have to go; I know how busy you are," he says in an effort to avoid any embarrassment.

"No, I would love to speak to your class." "Okay," he says politely, head bowed.

You gear up for your performance. After all, you have spoken to groups before. You stand up on your legs in court all the time. Talking is what you do for a living. What would the class like to hear? Maybe give a discussion of the First Amendment? Or, perhaps talk on the rights of children? You research your topic, you have notes, and you are prepared. Wearing your best suit, carrying your briefcase, off you go to your child's class.

The teacher greets you and explains that you will speak after Mark's Dad, the builder.

Mark's Dad has a tool belt, brings in some wood and proceeds to build a birdhouse—complete with turret and weather vane—in 5 minutes.

A hard act to follow, but you are prepared. Your child introduces you. You start your speech.

"Have you been on television?" asks one student. "No,"

"Oh," Your child wiggles in his seat.

"Do you carry tools? Like Mark's Dad?"

"No, I carry a briefcase."

"Oooh" they say. Your child wiggles some more.

"Do you build stuff?" asks a voice from the back of the room. You suspect the questioner is Mark.

"No, I research the law and write briefs."

"Oooooh," they say. Your child has about disappeared under his desk.

Finally, the teacher says, "Thank you, Ms. Lawyer."

Your child walks you to the door and the ordeal is over for both of you. The class moves on to Sally's Mom, who will show them how to make an origami bird.

The teenage years are no picnic when you have a lawyer for a parent. First of all, lawyers have strange senses of humor. They tell weird stories and they tell them anywhere—in front of your friends, their parents, and their friends. People look at them and wonder how they can believe that the fact that little Johnny, sent to live with his Aunt Tillie who placed him in a fancy private school where he proceeded to teach the other little boys socially unacceptable behavior, is hilarious.

Then there is the questioning. Lawyer parents ask annoying questions. Where are you going? Why? Who are going with? What time will you be home? Do I need to call the other parents?

Other parents ask those questions, but lawyer parents demand answers.

They will start their cross-examination with "Isn't it true that..." They call the other parents. And, if you end up in trouble for some transgression or another, they bring in several lawyers to straighten out the mess, causing you even more humiliation. Nothing is simple for lawyer parents.

Going through life with a lawyer parent is not easy. On the other hand, they do know how to read, research, and write. They also know how to argue. They will cause you to think and have reasons for your conclusions. They will force you to clarify the issue of a situation. While they do not drive trucks, carry neat tools or build anything, they are handy to have around when a problem arises. They will take it on, protect your rights and stand in your corner all your life.

Why do We do That?

National Lawyer Day

February is the longest shortest month of the year. Although it is only 28 days, 29 in a leap year, it is a month that lasts forever. The days are short and we rarely see the sun. We are ready for spring. We want to leave the house without putting on boots, gloves, hats, scarves and long winter coats. We want to come into court free of all those clothes. Once we add the briefcase filled with heavy files, the palm pilot and its accoutrements, the cellphone, the yellow legal pad complete with notes from long forgotten hearings and the writing instruments, we are sorely burdened. We yearn for the freedom and freshness that comes with spring.

In the meantime, we must live through February. There are numerous holidays in February to help us along. We start with Groundhog Day on February 2nd. We pray for clouds. If the sun shines and the groundhog sees his shadow, he scurries back into his hole to sleep for six more weeks. This means, of course, the delay of spring. A cloudy day and Mr. Punxsutawney Phil stays out and spring is around the corner. So we start out the month wanting more gloom.

We move on to Valentine's Day, February 14th. Presidents' Day is February 19th. The establishment of that day cheated us out of Lincoln's birthday (February 12th) and Washington's Birthday (February 22nd) as time off from the practice of law. Let us take all three days to praise and remember past presidents.

I suggest we add another holiday to help us get through the month: National Lawyer Day. Not Law Day celebrated in May and upon which many of us work, but a day to honor lawyers. Establishing a holiday requires considerable thought and planning. Setting up a holiday to honor lawyers would undoubtedly require extraordinary thought and planning.

Most holidays have colors associated with them. What colors can we associate with lawyers? A quick glance around a courtroom revealed gray, navy blue and black with a touch of red. One disgruntled person suggested gold to represent money. Let us use red for cheeriness and

Why do We do That?

black for black letter law and black robes. Red and black are good strong colors.

National Lawyer Day should have special candy. How about candy in the shape of gavels, scales of justice, palm pilots, cellphones and briefcases? That would work. We could have Pez dispensers designed to represent judges, lawyers or clients.

We need T-shirts emblazoned with "National Lawyer Day—take your lawyer to lunch." Or, "Have you thanked your lawyer recently?"

And flowers; we need flowers. There are plenty of red flowers. It might be harder to find black flowers. There are deep purple, almost black, irises. And this writer has heard of, but never seen, black orchids. There is, I am sure, a clever horticulturist out there who will find a way to create lawyer-like flowers. They will be expensive.

Lastly, we need a parade. What should be its theme? We could celebrate famous cases and their attorneys. The OJ trial, for example, or a tobacco case. Since we are into reality television, we could have a float entitled "When is it all right to eat your neighbor?" How about a Reasonable Doubt or a proximate cause theme? Or one entitled "My Favorite Tort."

The Capital Steps can march with their briefcases. The attorneys can walk in the parade to receive the adulation of their grateful clients. Bar associations could sponsor floats. A float honoring the judges would be appropriate.

What day of the month should be designated National Lawyer Day? I suggest a Friday, giving the weekend to recover from the celebration. If we refrain from work on all the holidays now available in February, add National Lawyer Day and one day of the four weekends of the month as a day of rest, we would only have to face the heavy clothes and the equipment of our profession fourteen days (fifteen days during a leap year) of the month. That is doable. That would make February truly the shortest month of the year. Now, what can we do about March?

What To Do If...

You find yourself agreeing with a John Grisham character that it is time to leave the practice of law. It is over. No more. No more ringing phones, no more needy clients, no more money dances by the mailbox, no more concerns. Off to [insert the dream destination of your choice].

Before closing the office door, some wrapping up must be done. **First,** call the State Bar (to which you have been paying money lo these many years) for advice on what to do with all those files. Follow their directions.

Second, arrange for the garage sale. Run an ad in Res Ipsa Loquitur or your local paper announcing the date, time and place. Walk through your office placing a little price sticker on each item, and taking a stab at an appropriate price for it. On sale day, wear casual clothes; assemble your cash box, a favorite chair and a cooler filled with the beverage of your choice. Place yourself comfortably by the door to the office, greet those entering, take the money of those leaving and enjoy the day.

Next, write the obituary. Here is a suggested obit:

Deceased. Beloved practice of J. Attorney. Age: many years. Closed this day following many battles for the rights of others. It is survived by numerous satisfied and one, maybe two, not-so-satisfied clients. A memorial service will be held at the home of J. Attorney on April 26, 2000. Please bring a "passing" dish.

Finally, plan for the memorial service. The memorial service declares that a death has occurred. It commemorates the life that has been lived. It offers friends, family and clients the opportunity to pay tribute to the deceased practice. So, a little planning is necessary.

What to do with the remains? What are the remains? The bar card is the one tangible piece of evidence of our existence as attorneys. Select a coffin for the bar card. A shoebox will do nicely. Line it with satin or velvet. Place the card on a little satin pillow. Some cultures adorn the "body" with amulets for future use. You might consider placing a yellow legal pad and a pen in the box to assist the card in its next life.

Why do We do That?

It is probably not necessary to decorate the outside of the box. A simple label: "Here lies the bar card of J. Attorney. RIP" could be affixed with tape. Place the coffin in the front parlor or other prominent place in your home for viewing. A few pictures of you in action might be appropriate.

Cremation or burial? Cremation is viewed by some as liberating the spirit of the deceased. Certainly your spirit will be liberated with the demise of the card. In winter, cremation might be the best solution. The ground is hard, it is cold and no one wants to go outside. If you have a fireplace, use it for the cremation. If not, a barbecue grill could be called into service. This would force folks to go outside, but only briefly.

The service prior to the cremation also needs to be planned. It is possible to call an acting school to hire mourners who will wail and grieve. Not to your liking?

A more conservative approach would be to ask people to say a few words about the practice of law.

Examples: "The Law: It has honoured us, may we honour it." (Webster) Or "Wrest once the law to your authority: To do a great right, do a little wrong." (Shakespeare) On Lawyers: "It is not, what a lawyer tells me I may do; but what humanity, reason, and justice, tell me I ought to do." (E. Burke)

Or, the line we all know so well: "The first thing we do, let's kill all the lawyers." (Shakespeare)

Following the lengthy eulogies, the assigned pallbearers can carry the "coffin" to the fireplace for disposal. Carefully placing the coffin on its funeral pyre you light the fire. A toast might be in order (see above for suggested words). A ceremonial tossing of the paper cups into the grill or fireplace would be appropriate. Once the remains are reduced to ashes, they can be scattered to the four winds in your backyard.

Ring. Ring. "Attorney J? This is Mrs. Gotbucks. I was referred to you by a former satisfied and happy client. My problem is...."

You are off and running. Back to the law. All other plans are canceled. For as Oliver Wendell Holmes said, "The life of the law has not been logic; it has been experience." When all is said and done, we do enjoy the experience.

The Lawyer In Court

Waiting 101

Law schools do a reasonably good job of teaching us the law. They do not, however, give us any direction on how to wait. As we all know, much of the practice of law in the courts is waiting. There is waiting, waiting, and more waiting. Then you're on. Then more waiting or off to another court at break-neck speed, because, of course, you are late due to so much waiting, only to wait some more. The question becomes what to do with this unstructured time. How can we make it profitable?

Most of us carry files with us under the mistaken and idealistic belief that we will actually work on those files. Attorneys have been observed reading files. One attorney was seen this past year, head down, eyes glazed over, staring at the computer screen, fingers flying. It can be assumed that one of two things was taking place: (a) he was working on a file or (b) he was playing a computer game. Whether (a) or (b), he was totally absorbed with his task. It is suspected that those attorneys with palm pilots are not really putting in court dates or making notes, but are playing solitaire.

Many of us are waiting for clients. You can tell who we are by the expectant look on our faces when the elevator doors open or we hear the fall of footsteps in the hall. Some of us can be seen in the hall, on the phone-calling clients. "What are you doing at home?" Or we call the office in the hopes the client called with a reason why he/she is late. When it becomes clear that the client is not coming, we start planning our request for an adjournment rather than a bench warrant in criminal cases, or we begin back-pedaling in civil cases. Our creative skills are called into play.

If, on the other hand, we find the client, we can move on to planning what we are going to say on behalf of that client. We review our arguments, looking for flaws. There are none. We negotiate with the opposite side. We strive for resolution if at all possible. We posture. We talk to our client. When we think we have a plan, we settle down for serious waiting.

Now we are on the ready line, so we talk to our peers. We catch up on the news of the day. We discuss interesting points of law. We listen to other arguments both on and off the record. We think "Well, good point." The judge shoots it down. "Guess not." Judge accepts it. "All right, I'll try that sometime." We get bored and restless.

We read. What do we read? The following have been seen in court. Newspapers, some legal, but mostly others such as Auction News, Ann Arbor News, New York Times; magazines include sports, gardening, or general interest. Strangely, there are no fashion magazines; we must not be fashionable. Novels of various types are spotted tucked discreetly in files. They are of the short, entertainment fiction variety. Whatever we read must not require a lot of attention, as we must listen for our turn. When called, we leap into action.

The most difficult waiting is the waiting for a jury verdict. During the waiting time, we first go over the trial. Then we review our closing argument. Did I remember this point? What about that point? Was it included?

It has been said that there are three closing arguments. The first is the argument we practice in the car on our way to court; the second is the one we actually give to the jury; and third, the most brilliant by far, is the one we give in the car on our way home. So we wait and second-guess ourselves. We try to work and we wait.

Clearly, law school did not prepare us for this waiting business. Maybe it is time to launch a campaign to have Waiting 101 added to all law school curricula. Write to the Deans. Demand a course on the creative use of this time. Or, learn to enjoy that unstructured time and not feel guilty.

Fun Time at Ye Olde Courthouse

The Courthouse to the lawyers that frequent its hallowed halls is a house of courts. We come in, go through security, smile, chat or frown, and scurry up the stairs to find our clients and the court to which we are assigned.

We see the courtrooms as arenas: places to do battle. Those battles are tense. There are winners and there are losers. If our client is the loser, we have a loser and an unhappy client. If our client is the winner, we may still have an unhappy client because, of course they won, we were superfluous and we charge too much anyway. So we deal with a lot of unhappiness.

We tend to forget the other, more pleasant departments of the courthouse. Or, at least the departments that left the courthouse to exist in the new and perhaps more pleasant digs across the street. As some of you may have noticed, in the course of remodeling, the Register of Deeds and the Vital Records sections of the County Clerk department are no longer in this building. At least those offices were not battlefields.

Vital Records is a wealth of services and information. Going on a world tour? Go to Vital Records to apply for your passport or if you need a birth certificate to get the passport, it's the same department. Planning a wedding? Apply for the marriage license, wait three days and off you go to your wedding. If you want a judge to marry you, it used to be you could go up the stairs with your license in hand and it could be done.

Suppose you have decided the time has come to leave the practice of law to open a widget factory. Register that business at the same office and you will get all kinds of fun mail. Want to find out about your ancient relatives? Go there to search. Alas, Vital Records has left the building.

The Register of Deeds has also left. The services provided by that division could often settle conflicts. Suppose for some reason you want to know who owned your house. Search the records at the Register of Deeds. Those records include deeds, mortgages, discharges of mortgage,

Why do We do That?

death certificates, liens, trusts, powers of attorney–any document that relates to your property is filed in that office. Or that relates to your ancestor's property–a source of information for a genealogist. Another nice division has left the building.

What can fill the space left as a result of the departure of those divisions? A survey of the lawyers who frequent the courthouse came up with some suggestions. All agreed. We need to bring cheer into the building. We need to have fun. We need to relax. We are sorely stressed.

Now this writer must admit that some of the suggestions were practical. Some wanted a day- care center. Not a bad suggestion considering that Family Court will soon include Juvenile Court clients who tend to bring their own and other people's children to court with them. Those children get restless and sometimes run up and down the halls, creating noise and confusion and striking fear in the hearts of the adults. They need a place to be contained while the adults decide their fates. A day-care center would be most welcome. Or how about a client care center where we can drop off our clients? They could relieve their tension and anxiety by playing violent video games.

Another practical suggestion is to use the space for a health club. As lawyers generally do not spend their time in physical activity, a health club is a good proposal. We can use the facility to work out, becoming healthier and thus better able to do battle. Add a spa and/or a yoga studio and the picture is complete.

Some wanted pool tables. Pool tables provide many happy hours of fun. Tournaments can be arranged and scores posted. Perhaps small wagers can be placed, adding to the competition.

Dartboards with space for the appropriate picture of your choice can be hung, providing another source of entertainment.

For the younger lawyers who are unaware of the pleasures of pool, billiards or darts, video games can be installed. Participants in video games appear to be totally engrossed with the battles they are waging. In this way the cares of the legal world could be avoided for a few happy hours.

A coffee house was suggested. Other suggestions were a yogurt bar, a hot dog stand or perhaps a pub with appropriate drinks and pub meals. Since in today's world food and books go together, a bookstore can be built. A nice one with shelves and shelves of interesting books to wile away the hours as we wait for clients or court appearances.

Why do We do That?

A fortuneteller might come in handy. We could ascertain the outcome of our cases and ease our minds. It is always nice to know the future. One wag suggested a massage parlor. A movie theater complete with first run movies, popcorn and soft drinks is a pleasant thought.

As you can see, the possibilities are endless. We need a committee to assist the powers that be with the decision-making. They need our input on the best use of the recently vacated space. This writer has complete confidence in the ability of a committee of lawyers to create an attractive alternative to more courtrooms and more offices. It should be remembered, however, that regardless of what we put in the newly created Lawyer's Lair, it must, like all good lairs, have a back door.

Why do We do That?

Why do We do That?

Black's Law Meets Shakespeare

We are in an era of technology. The theatrical quality of the courtroom is enhanced by that technology. Evidence can be electronically presented. People or evidence can be displayed on 40" television screens that would be the envy of any sports bar. All this technology is being used in an effort to gain the attention of the media-blitzed jurors and win the case.

So, fine—you know how to use these technological marvels. Or you have a twenty- something assistant that knows how to use these things. But to the judge, the jury and your client, you are the most important communication tool in the courtroom.

Professor Annette Masson, of the University of Michigan Department of Theater and Drama, says, "The human being is the most important part of communication." Technology is merely an assistant. The trial attorney, like an actor in a play, still must use voice, eyes, body, imagination, mind and will to persuade the jury—and should appear comfortable with that role.

There are attorneys who are completely at home in the courtroom. They are at ease under any attack. They are in tune with their bodies. Their voice makes the jury want to keep listening. Many of us, however, suffer from common, ordinary stage fright. Our knees shake, our mouths get dry or our minds go blank when the judge sustains our opponent's tenth objection. Our voices sound tiny or overbearing.

What to do?

Do what actors have done since the days of the Bard of Avon. Breathe. Actors know that proper breathing helps them face the crises by soothing jangled nerves and slowing down the nervous system, allowing them to regain control of themselves and the situation. Proper breathing can cure almost all signs of stage fright. Good breathing is a source of agile voices, stamina and energy, concentration, flexibility and openness. Like athletes training for a competition, actors use breathing exercises to control themselves and their voices. There are simple breathing, relaxation, concentration and vocal production techniques that we can learn and practice to improve our performance.

We also need to be aware of our bodies. Aware of how we move through space. Do we rattle change in our pockets or pace or move from side to side? Do we know what to do with our hands and arms or are they in the way? A little acting training can chase those bad habits away. A few physical warm-ups before trial can help.

After we practice our breathing and do vocal and physical warm-ups, we must practice the story we are about to tell the jury. The client's position should be shaped into a tale the jury can follow. We want their minds, imaginations and hearts to respond to our opening statement. How do we get to those minds? Again look to actors who "own" the story of their character. They use different methods to get into the story, such as miming the events of the story to find the dramatic high points, or taking a mind's eye walk through the entire story.

Attorneys can get into the subjective side of their cases by writing down their first impressions and gut reactions after the first meeting with the client, or by telling the "story" to an associate in one minute, or by thinking back to his/her own life to a similar situation to find the emotional elements. We need to put aside our reasoning objective left-brain and let our subjective right-brain out for a bit of work.

Actors, like lawyers, plan a set of objectives to be achieved during the course of the play.

These objectives must be accomplished to convince the audience that the conclusion of the play is the right conclusion. This plan is a performance strategy.

A trial needs both a legal strategy and a performance strategy. The legal strategy consists of the facts and the law. The performance strategy is designed to engage the audience or, in the case of the courtroom, the judge, the jury and the gallery and to gain their trust. That strategy begins at the door of the courtroom. The legal and the performance strategies should merge, ensuring that the lawyer, the witnesses and the audience all know the objective. If asked, "What is this trial about?" the audience should be able to answer the question with a single sentence.

All of this would be easy if we had scripts. But we do not. The opposing side has its own strategies. So, like actors, we must be flexible. If an actor forgets his lines or gets the wrong response to his line, he must improvise. If the witness falls apart, we must improvise. Being at ease with ourselves and with the courtroom gives us the ability to think on our feet and be flexible enough to change direction mid-stream. Maybe an acting program tailored for attorneys could help those of us who want to strengthen or feel more comfortable with our courtroom performances.

Are there acting workshops for attorneys? Yes, of course there are—in New York or California or Chicago. None where you are? Professor Annette Masson at the University of Michigan assures this writer one could easily be put together. Any takers?

Why do We do That?

Voir Dire Made Easy

Many of us at one time or another have studied the jury selection process in great detail. We have gone to seminars, read books and, if our client is prosperous enough, we have even had mock trials counseled by experts in jury selection. We learn that the perfect juror for a widowed client suing a large corporation for damages for the wrongful death of her husband is a dependent disenfranchised woman with children. As prosecutor, we might select conservative businessmen when faced with a white-collar criminal defendant.

We are told that to win our case we should create a personal portrait of our perfect juror. We read the jury questionnaires in an effort to find the type of person who, in a case relating to violence or embezzlement or simply unfairness, would feel sympathetic to our client. The other side will do the same. We watch the panel of jurors as they wait, we watch them as they walk to jury box and watch how they interact with fellow jurors, if at all.

When it comes to voir dire, which means, "to speak the truth," we are advised to watch our questioning techniques for their effect on the jurors; to analyze the kinds of questions we ask to see what we really get from the answers; and to look into new areas of questioning that will get more insightful information.

All this in an instant while on our feet, looking casual and friendly as we are advised to do, selling our side of the case after arguing with the judge and the other attorney about who and how the questions will be asked.

Fear not. The answer is at hand. A recent study on food hedonics, which roughly translates to the pleasures associated with food, has all the answers. Dr. Alan R. Hirsch, who heads the Smell and Taste Treatment and Research Foundation, conducted a Snack Food Hedonics and Personality study that tells us what we eat is who we are.

"I think food makes more sense as a window to one's unconscious than, say, a Rorschach test," says the good Doctor. What did the study find?

Why do We do That?

The following:

Potato chip lovers

Those who love potato chips are ambitious, successful, high achievers. They enjoy the rewards and trimmings of their success—at home and at the office. They seek nothing but the best in those around them. They are easily frustrated and indignant at life's inconveniences. They are furious when required to wait in line or wait for a call to a courtroom. They are prepared adversaries.

Tortilla chip eaters

The tortilla chip eaters are perfectionists, always expecting only the best from themselves.

They will redo a project until it is absolutely right. The lover of tortilla chips is a stickler for punctuality and tries never to be late. They carry the weight of the world on their shoulders, making sure all is well with finances, health, children, car repairs and household chores. A person you might want on a deserted island, but not on a jury where your client has done something less than perfect.

Pretzel preferrers

Lively and energetic, those who prefer pretzels crave novelty and are easily bored with routine. They are excited by challenge—whether it is at work, sports or home. They thrive in the world of abstract concepts and tend to lose interest in the day-to-day world. They will initiate new projects without having completed the last. They make decisions based on intuition and emotion. A pretzel lover would do well on short trials but would not be happy with a long drawn-out affair unless, of course, it presented an intellectual challenge.

Snack cracker snackers

Snack cracker lovers are thoughtful, logically rather than intuitively oriented; their decisions are reasoned and not based on emotions. They avoid confrontation so as not to hurt the feelings of others. They have many diverse interests and are involved in a multitude of projects simultaneously, all competing for their time and attention. Snack cracker lovers would not be the ones to hold out against the rest of the jurors.

Cheese curl munchers

Cheese curl lovers have a fine sense of right and wrong, yet treat all whom they meet fairly.

They have integrity and are always prepared. At work, at play or at home, no detail is left undone. With their sense of right and wrong and because you are in the right, the cheese curl lover may be the perfect juror for you.

Meat Snackers

Gregarious and social, meat-snack lovers are at their best in the company of others. They are generous and will make extraordinary self-sacrifices to please. Meat-snack lovers are loyal and true friends who can always be trusted. If you get them on your client's side they will stick with him or her through the whole trial.

Conclusions

Should your jury be all one snack food or do certain combinations work well together? The research says:

Potato chip munchers are most compatible with someone who prefers potato chips or pretzels.

Tortilla chip eaters should only team up with tortilla chip lovers

Pretzel lovers are compatible with potato chips, pretzels or cheese curls diners Snack cracker fans should hook up with pretzel fans

Cheese curl devourers are good with potato chip and tortilla chip lovers.

Meat-snack snackers are suited to those who prefer potato chips or meat snacks.

So—out with the jury forms. A simple form with name, address and snack food preference will tell us all we need to know.

Why do We do That?

A Lagniappe—Something Extra

New Orleans, Louisiana was the site of the National Romance Writers Conference this year so writer-daughter and I made the trek to that city in mid-July. Writer-daughter uses the conference to make connections and learn new stuff. I use the conference to escape the every day practice of law and explore new worlds. There is much to explore in New Orleans.

New Orleans or The Big Easy has as its credo "Let the Good Times Roll." There are drive-through daiquiri shops, cafes open 24-7, and plastic "go-cups" for folks wishing to take their libation with them as they stroll up and down Bourbon Street. The food, Creole and Cajun, is prepared by some of the best chefs in the country. The music, live, available and of many varieties, leads to dancing in the streets. And, of course, tourists and locals celebrate the famous Mardi Gras with its magnificent floats and days of fun and laughter.

While the living inhabitants of this 300-year-old tropical city live life with gusto, the dead also make their presence known. First there is the matter of keeping the dead buried. Some of you may remember law school and the case of floating coffins. The people have solved that problem with aboveground crypts housed in large ornate cemeteries aptly called the Cities of the Dead.

The problem of space is solved with the continual reuse of the tombs. Local law states that a body shall be interred for a year and a day before it can be moved—long enough to work a natural cremation. If space is needed, the ashes are placed in an ash pit beneath or behind the crypt with other family members long gone. This practice could cause one to ponder one's intra- family relationships more carefully during life, knowing what the future could bring.

Louisiana law is based on the Napoleonic Code, not the British Common law. The differences between the practice of law there and elsewhere in the United States make it necessary to find a local attorney to navigate the complexities of that state's peculiar laws and practices. Then there is the matter of voodoo. The local attorneys have the knowledge of the local law and "a lagniappe" or "something extra" in the form of voodoo. A trip to the local New Orleans Historic Voodoo Museum and gift shop revealed several "Spells for good luck in court and other legal matters."

To make things go their way, the local attorneys can try these spells:

The night before you appear in court, burn four black candles, four purple candles and four white candles, anointing them first with High John the Conqueror Oil and then roll the candles in Helping Hand powdered incense. This should make the testimony of your foe unbelievable to the judge.

Before you go to sleep, sprinkle the four corners of your bedroom with peace water and carry a High John the Conqueror root with you until the trial is over.

When you receive legal papers, you must fold the papers four times and then place them in a small red flannel bag. Add some five-finger grass, close the bag with black yarn, and anoint it with four drops of geranium oil. Sleep with the bag for four nights before you see the judge, meditating on and visualizing the desired result. The judge will be unable to resist ruling your way.

(For the Defense Attorneys among us) To control a Prosecuting Attorney, take a plain piece of white paper and write the name of the attorney three times and then write your name three times across his/her name. Put this paper in your left shoe, then mix 3 drops of Rose oil, Verbena oil, Lavender oil and Black Arts oil; shake well and rub the bottom of your left foot with this mixture before going to court.

The best way to win is to go to an authentic Voodoo practitioner and have them make a powerful court case Gris-Gris bag, a small bag filled with herbs and oils and tied at the top. Be sure to bring the name of the judge and each person sitting on the jury if at all possible. Write all the names on a piece of parchment paper. Be careful not to misspell any of the names. Carry your Gris-Gris bag in the right pocket if you are male or on the left side if female. Now you are ready for court.

All the ingredients needed to create the spells can be found in the gift shop of the museum, or other voodoo shops around the city. It is not at all clear how this works if both sides are using "a lagniappe." Which spell controls?

Perhaps if one is working with the Napoleonic Code one needs "a lagniappe." For those of us working in common law states, we should probably stick to our common methods and leave the "something extra" to the attorneys of Louisiana.

Why do We do That?

Artists and Lawyers Connect the Dots

Recently I was in Chicago with writer-daughter who was presenting a paper to an International Education Society. Finding the conversation of those folks less interesting than the war stories told by lawyers, I walked to Chicago's wonderful Art Museum, a mere two blocks from our hotel, for a little enlightenment and entertainment.

I entered, walking between the magnificent lions guarding the entrance to the museum, and made my way to the ticket window where I was pleased to discover that the more mature among us, which includes me, paid a smaller entrance fee. I got a map and was off to the new Modern Wing of the museum, passing through Asian art, which, while interesting, did not speak to me.

In the modern wing I found the jewel of the museum, A Sunday Afternoon on the Island of La Grande Jatte by Georges Seurat. For those who took the Art History 101 course designed for non-art majors, you know this is an enormous canvas (seven by ten feet) depicting Parisian city dwellers gathered at a park on La Grande Jatte (literally, "the big platter"), an island in the River Seine. All kinds of people stroll, lounge, sail, and fish in the park. Seurat rendered his subject by placing tiny, precise brush strokes of different colors close to one another so that they blend at a distance. Stepping close to the painting, I saw the tiny dots. The style was labeled Pointillism by the art critics of the time (1884-86); with a touch of derision, I might add. Stepping back, the dots came together and I saw the wonderful Sunday afternoon scene.

In preparation for the final work, Seurat visited the park many times, making more than 30 sketches before beginning the final piece, which took over two years to create. Sitting on the bench absorbing the painting and watching other visitors step close and then step back, I was reminded of how lawyers use dots of information to create a picture for the judge or the jury.

Sometimes they only need to use a few dots, other times they must spend many hours discovering the facts and putting them side-by-side to present their case. Like the artist, they are depicting reality in their own way for their own purposes.

Listening to the museum visitors, I heard "Look at the little girl, she's the only one running. Did you see the boats on the river? The painting is kind of fuzzy, isn't it? Is that because of the little dots?" Like juries listening to facts, each visitor saw something a little different, which, of course, is what makes the painting interesting. And, what makes trials interesting.

Unlike the artists, who are probably content to have their creation viewed and interpreted as the viewer will, lawyers connect the dots to create their own particular picture. They use their dots to influence. They can create an ogre or a teddy bear, depending on which side of the painting they are standing.

The end result, however, is still in the eyes of the beholder. The artist and the lawyer are both left with the interpretation of the work by the jury or critic standing back to view all the dots as they merge. The artists may be encouraged or discouraged by the critic's words. But for the lawyers, the end result, the final picture they create, can result in a happy or unhappy client, in justice or injustice, depending on how the jury connects the dots. Both artists and lawyers, however, will emerge from the challenge of creation ready to take on the next painting and connect its dots. They know no other way; they must move forward.

Techno-Trial in a Techno-Court

Consider the following scene:

A trial begins. The participants blink into existence on computer monitors. They are not in the same room, the same building or the same city. They can be anywhere. Judge, counsel, parties, witnesses and jury appear in virtual form on each person's monitor. Witnesses presenting evidence are questioned by distant attorneys. A real-time, multi-media record is instantly available. When a sidebar conference is needed, the jury is switched out of the loop. They can do what they want in their own homes. The public can follow the proceedings on the Internet. If the appellate court is needed, it can directly monitor the proceedings.

Or, consider this more simplified version:

Sassy Sally Public decides to fight her traffic ticket. She schedules her court appearance with the court using the World Wide Web. If she can't get to the central computer kiosk in the mall, she can use the computer on her desk to join the virtual courtroom. The judge and the traffic officer appear in windows on the screen. Each can be in a different location. Sally has her say; the Officer has her say. The Judge rules.

This sounds like the Holodeck on the Enterprise of Star Trek fame. Is the technology here for a virtual trial in a virtual courtroom, meaning that no one is in the same place at the same time? Maybe not at this moment. Could it be accomplished? Oh, it appears so. Is this writer ready for such technology? Probably not. Can either you or I become ready for the technology? Presumably.

The techno-trial of today generally comes to the courtroom in a more pedestrian form. Technologically adept attorneys walk it in. Computers are brought in to present evidence electronically. Use of Power Point adds interest and perhaps more appeal to the material being presented to the jury. The computers are used to find cases to support arguments. Michigan Court Rules can be pulled up on a Palm Pilot as needed. When the trial is over, the technology used goes out the door with the attorney and the courtroom is back to its quiet Twentieth Century self.

But not for long. Local judges are attempting to force at least one of their courtrooms into the 21st century. What could that mean?

DOAR Communications, Inc. has created a technologically advanced Federal Courtroom in Orlando, which includes:

1. Multiple high-resolution display monitors for the judge, court clerk, court reporter, witness and each counsel table. The jury box has 10 individual flat screen monitors that can be angled so that all jurors can see the screen.

2. The court has four 40" high-definition fluid plasma screen monitors. The monitors are used for remote witness and evidence presentation.

3. The podium holds more than a dusty shelf with the Advice of Rights forms and a microphone. The DOAR podium is the 'control center' for all the video/digital display within the courtroom. It provides full support for laptop presentations.

4. Teleconferencing, which means a witness across the country or across town can be brought up on the 40" screen placed behind the witness chair. He is sworn in and testifies as if he were in the courtroom. The jury, the attorneys, the court personnel and the gallery see the witness. The remote witness sees a multi-frame TV image of the speaker and sections of the courtroom as well as a comprehensive image of the entire courtroom. Evidence can be displayed using document cameras or computers.

The Twenty-first Century is upon us. The technology is out there. It may soon be in every village and hamlet. The issue is not whether these changes will occur, but when. We will adapt after we debate the many questions such technology raises. The debate and the adaptation may be rocky at times, but the end result should prove most exciting.

The Law of Change

"I am not buying a car without a steering wheel," I said to my grandson, Collin, when he informed me that Mercedes-Benz was designing a car controlled by a joystick. "That is too weird."

I am not sure who could drive that car, certainly not my generation, perhaps a generation as yet unborn. The car, it is reported, will not be available until 2028. By that time, I guess anyone interested in it will be accomplished at video games and joysticks.

Each generation grows up with its own culture and its own name. Baby Boomers (born 1946-1964) are said to be outer driven, Gen X (1965-1976) reactive, and Millenials (1977-) are inner driven. What unites those generations is their ability to adapt to change.

As each one comes along it adds to the body of knowledge and technology that supports it. Some of us are left behind, but most of us learn new skills with amazing speed. We go "on-line" to "surf the net" or to check our "email;" terms and experiences unheard of by most of us twenty years ago.

Fortunately, we can select the technology we wish to learn. While I am presently incapable of "text messaging" on my cell phone, I suspect I will have to learn in the future if I wish to communicate with my grandchildren

The law, unlike us mortals, is not selective but adapts to all the changes in society. The law of homicide through negligent driving, for example, goes back to English common law in the horse and buggy days. Hale's Pleas of the Crown (1716) said, "...it is the duty of any man who drives any carriage, to drive it with such care and caution as to prevent, as far as in his power, any accident or injury that may occur." The same duty of care will apply to a person driving a car with a joystick.

Legal scholars have long recognized the ability of the law to change. Aeschylus said, "The laws of a state change with the changing times." Seven Against Thebes, 476 B.C.

More recently, Roscoe Pound noted, "Law must be stable, and yet it

can not stand still." Modern Legal Glossary, 1983.

And, of course, Thomas Jefferson, that great advocate of change, said, "Laws and institutions must go hand in hand with the progress of the human mind."

While technology may outdistance laws for a time, we can be sure the law will catch up and adapt. Generations too will change, but again the law will adjust. This ability to transform is its beauty and its strength.

Drive-Through Sentencing

The courts in Washtenaw County were, and perhaps still are, part of a pilot project called the Unified Trial Court. A unified court appears to mean that judges are fungible. Judge A = Judge B
= Judge C. It also means that District Court judges act as Circuit Court judges under certain circumstances. One of those circumstances occurs in the area of criminal law.

For those of you who don't practice in this area, a short (very short) explanation of criminal procedure is necessary. For those of you who do practice in criminal law, skip the explanation. Unless, of course, you are like most lawyers who read everything that comes before their eyes.

At any rate, in felony level criminal procedure, a preliminary examination is a beginning step in the criminal process. The preliminary examination is held in the District Court before a District Court judge. The purpose of the examination is to determine whether there is probable cause to send the matter to the Circuit Court, which has jurisdiction over felonies. The District Court has jurisdiction over misdemeanors. If there is enough evidence the matter is bound over to the Circuit Court for a trial.

Often it is clear that the defendant is going to plead guilty to the charge so a plea agreement is negotiated at the prelim. In the past, the procedure was to waive the preliminary examination, agree to the bind over to the circuit court judge assigned to the case. That judge would accept the plea and sentence the defendant.

In an effort to move matters along in a more efficient manner, it was decided to vest District Court judges with Circuit Court powers so they could take pleas. A Circuit Court judge would then sentence the defendant after reviewing the pre-sentence report created by the probation officer. The defendant has to agree to this procedure and must sign a waiver, waiving his right to have the same judge accept his plea and set the sentence.

The purpose behind the old policy, which applied to both trial-based and plea-based convictions, was to ensure that the judge who heard the evidence at plea would sentence the defendant based on the circumstances established at the time of the plea.

"When a judge who has not heard the evidence at the plea-taking sentences the defendant, the sentence may not be tailored to fit the particular circumstances of the case and the offender."

People v Pierce, 158 Mich App 113, 116 (1987). Per case law, a sentencing judge should be familiar with the circumstances of the case and the offender.

Why? Does it really matter? After all, we are a fast-paced society. We have drive- through banking, food, prescriptions, coffee, etc. You name a need and someone will create a drive- through to satisfy that need. Because we have a need to speed up the criminal justice system, we now have drive-through sentencing. You give your plea at one window and pick up your sentence at another. The procedure is easy, fast, efficient.

In some cases, that may be all right. Admittedly, in some rare cases, it might be better if the judge never saw your client. But in other cases, it may be important for the sentencing judge to see and hear the defendant while he enters his guilty plea. An impression, however slight, is created. That impression, along with the circumstances of the plea, influences the sentence. Does this person seem remorseful? Does he or she accept responsibility for his or her acts?

We know that impressions are made quickly, often in 20-30 seconds. Those few seconds could assure that the judge has complete information about your client, not merely words on a page drafted by someone else, but an unabridged picture. A picture that will ensure a proper individualized sentence is set. An individualized sentence tailored to the particular circumstances of the case and the offender. An individualized sentence that looks at the protection of society and the rehabilitation of the offender. Maybe, it is possible that not all sentencing should be "drive- through" sentencing.

Juvenile Courts: Then and Now

The nineteenth century was described as an age of institutions. Among the many institutions created during those times were Houses of Refuge, Houses of Reformation or Reform Schools for children. These institutions, the first of which were created in New York State in 1824, were for children who had committed crimes, who were incorrigible or who presented other problems for their parents or the community but who were thought to be capable of being redirected toward productive lives.

Children, once convicted of a crime, were no longer placed in prisons with adults but were placed in the reform schools. Eventually communities became aware of other children who needed help due to neglect or abuse by their parents or guardians. Those children were also placed in Houses of Refuge. As a result of these concerns regarding the welfare of children, juvenile courts were established.

The first Juvenile Court was created in 1899 in Cook County, Illinois. The law was an act to "to regulate the treatment and control of dependent, neglected and delinquent children."   It created no new courts but provided that circuit court judges should designate one or more of their number to hear all juvenile cases, a juvenile courtroom should be separately provided and a separate record kept of the proceedings. Cook County was the only county in Illinois to establish a separate Juvenile Court.

The most important provision of the Illinois law was the concept that children who committed crimes were not to be considered criminals but were wards of the state and subject to the control of the Juvenile Court. The delinquent child was to receive the same care, custody and discipline as given to a neglected or abused child. Thus, great care was taken to eliminate in every way the idea of a criminal procedure.

Juvenile hearings were to be held in judges' chambers, which should be "clean, bright and cheerful with inspiring pictures on the wall depicting happy family and child life." Judges were told to use a gentle, pleasant voice and friendly demeanor. As the proceedings were not criminal in nature, no record was to be kept of the discussions. The official papers were to avoid the use of criminal terminology. Testimony should be taken without too many objections. And, of course, the child did not need a lawyer. If an attorney did appear, "the judge should deal tactfully with the attorney, even complimenting him on his work in the presence of his clients." In this way it was said, "the lawyer will accept the juvenile court approach and will assist the judge in developing a welfare program for the juvenile."

This was the standard for many years. A court for juvenile delinquents, whose purpose was to create up-standing members of society by offering treatment rather than punishment; a court for children abused or neglected by their parents where the parents could be provided with services in an effort to keep the family together. This was the standard in early June 1964, when Gerald Francis Gault and his friend, Ronald Lewis came home from school with nothing to do.

Bored, they called Mrs. Cook, a neighbor, on the telephone and made some remarks that were "of the irritatingly offensive, adolescent, sex variety." In re Gault, 387 U.S. 1 (1967).

On June 8, 1964, Gerald and Ronald were taken into custody by the Sheriff. No message was left at the home telling the parents, who were not present, of Gerald's arrest. When the parents learned that Gerald was in the detention home, they went to see him. At that point they were told of a hearing the next day June 9, 1964, at 3:00 p.m.

The hearing was held in the judge's chambers. Present were Gerald, his mother and brother and two probation officers. Mrs. Cook— remember Mrs. Cook? —was not there. No record was made of the hearing. As a result of what was said, Gerald was again placed in detention. He was released on June eleventh with no explanation. The family was told to be back in court on June 15, 1964, at 11:00 a.m. for further hearings on "Gerald's delinquency." Again Mrs. Cook was not present and no record was kept of the hearing. The probation officer presented a "referral report" which was not given to Gerald or his parents. At the end of the hearing, the judge committed Gerald as a juvenile delinquent to the State Industrial School "for a period of his minority [that is, until 21], unless sooner discharged by due process of law." Gerald was 15 at the time.

The US Supreme Court reversed the lower court stating "there is no place in our system of law for reaching a result of such tremendous consequences without ceremony..." The court held that juveniles were entitled to the constitutional guarantees of notice of charges, right to counsel, right to confrontation and cross-examination and the privilege against self-incrimination. The dissent, written by Mr. Justice Harlan, concluded " I very much fear that this Court, by imposing these rigid procedural requirements, may inadvertently have served to discourage efforts to find more satisfactory solutions for the problems of juvenile crime, and may thus now hamper enlightened development of the systems of juvenile courts." That was the final word in 1967.

Flash forward to 1996 when the law changed in Michigan. If a juvenile 14 years of age or older is accused of an act that if committed by an adult would be a felony, the assigned judge can decide to try the child as an adult.

In the 1800's in this country there were no juvenile courts. Children were tried and convicted in adult criminal courts. Parents who neglected their children were tried under the criminal laws. Then, as we have seen, there was a period of reform. Juvenile courts were created. Juvenile cases that came before the court were treated as non-criminal. After In re Gault, there were more cases upholding a juvenile's right to additional constitutional guarantees.

Now juveniles have the full protection of our constitution as they stand before a judge in the criminal court facing many of the same punishments given to adults. Is this progress? Justice Harlan may have been right.

Why do We do That?

The Lawyer In Society

The Law is Not Boring

I am taking a course in writing at Lansing Community College. At our first class, Mary, a professor at the college, sat next to me. When we exchanged names and professions, she said she thought the law was boring. I was taken aback and puzzled. I didn't understand how one could think a profession that has given us so much is boring. I thought of all the ways the law has made our lives more orderly, interesting and stimulating.

Because of the law:

Millions witnessed the peaceful transition of presidential power from George W. Bush to our 44th President, Barack Obama, the 26th lawyer president. Michelle Obama, also a lawyer, looked on as he took the oath of office. Thanks in part to his training in critical thinking during his years at Harvard Law; President Obama believes he is ready to accept the challenges of his new position and all it represents. I trust his presidency will not be dry or monotonous or boring.

Supreme Court Chief Justice Roberts gave us a moment to remember during the inauguration when, as he administered the oath to our president-elect, he misplaced the word 'faithfully   y.' For those who might be concerned, Mr. Obama is still President Obama as the law in   the form of the 20th amendment to our Constitution states that the new President assumes office at noon on January 20th regardless of a misplaced word. This simple ceremony was not tedious or lifeless.

Recently writer-daughter, Melissa, and I along with hundreds of others enjoyed a performance of the musical comedy, Legally Blonde, the story of Elle Woods's transformation by Harvard Law from ditsy blonde to self-confident young lawyer ready to become part of the legal community. The play, filled with law, law students, lawyers, music and dancing, was amusing and engaging. It was not dreary or unexciting.

Wonderful legal thrillers are written by lawyers such as John

Why do We do That?

Grisham and Scott Turow to entertain and inform and are enjoyed by millions of readers. The adventures of Patricia Cornwell's Kaye Scarpetta, a lawyer, doctor and medical examiner, are eagerly followed by legions of faithful readers who are neither uninterested nor indifferent to the problems Scarpetta faces and solves with her legally trained mind.

And then, of course, there are all the famous trials conducted by lawyers according to the law that shaped our thinking and changed lives. Think of the Salem Witchcraft Trials (1692), The Mutiny on the Bounty Courts-Martial (1807), and Lizzie Borden's trial in 1893; there is a poem about that one. More recently, Leopold and Loeb (1924), Chicago 7 trial (1969-70), Sam Sheppard Trials of 1954 and '66, Charles Manson (1970-71), McMartin Preschool (1987-90),

O.J. Simpson (1995), and Moussaoui (9/11) of 2006. Learned professors make lists and lists of famous trials. Writers research and write books about them and Hollywood makes movies of them. These trials are not humdrum or uninspiring. They and many others captured the interest of the nation and added excitement to our lives.

And, finally, last Saturday, the law enriched my life.

I received a check for $13.37 as part of LiPuma Class Action Settlement. This was a matter brought by ambitious lawyers who used the law to force American Express to pay for an unlawful action committed against an entire class of folks who were, like myself, thrilled to receive a check.

No, Mary, the law is not boring. It is fascinating, thrilling, and thought- provoking and sometimes frustrating, but it is rarely dull, monotonous or boring.

The Sun, a Game, and a Contract

The sun, in a cloudless sky, beamed down on 110,000 folks at the University of Michigan stadium in Ann Arbor. A sea of yellow from the maize shirts worn by thousands of Michigan fans smiled back at the sun.

The bands played their fight songs; the cheerleaders led the cheers; we yelled until we were hoarse. The sound reverberated around the oval stadium, now partially enclosed with skyboxes for those who believe they need more than the usual 18 inches of sitting space on the bleachers below.

Michigan—with its new coach known among some of the students and fans as Rich Rod, and a freshman quarterback named Tate Forcier, whose stellar performance has led to the expression "let the Forcier be with you,"—was playing Notre Dame. Fans on both sides, unable to sit still, stood for every play.

At halftime, Michigan was down three points, our passing and rushing yard gains were dismal, and we were not sure, but still willing, to cheer for our team. As I was sitting eating my ripe, red, Jonathon apple for the energy needed for the second half, the lady next to me— we'll call her Sharon—stood up and moved down a row with camera in hand and turned to take a picture of the young couple seated directly behind us.

"What are you doing?" asked her husband, Harry.

"I am taking their picture, they asked me to, and they want the scoreboard in background of the picture," she answered.

Sharon focused the camera and took one picture while the couple smiled. The young man asked her to take another picture and with that he faced the girl, went down on one knee, pulled a small white box out of his pocket, and asked, "Will you marry me?"

She gasped, her mouth open, her blue eyes wide, then beamed as she answered "yes." He opened the box and there nestled in white satin was a diamond engagement ring. He placed it on her finger. She cried.

Sharon snapped the pictures.

We cheered and spread the word up and down the rows.

Why do We do That?

We quickly learned that Harry and the bride-to-be graduated from the same high school in a small town in Ohio. The future husband purchased the engagement ring at a jewelry store located around the corner from Sharon and Harry's Toledo home. We agreed it is a small world. We also agreed that we should all be invited to the wedding. I suspect that will not happen.

Halftime ended, the teams flooded the field, and the battle began anew. It continued down to the final 11 seconds with Michigan behind 31-34, when quarterback Forcier went back for a pass, threw, and we waited. The ball flew through the air. Greg Mathews plucked it out of the sky in the end zone. Touchdown, Michigan. The kick was good. Final score 38-34.

The newly engaged couple did spend much of the second half on their respective cell phones sending the news far and wide. However, they watched and waited with the rest of us as the ball left Forcier's hand. They will remember that game for their own personal reasons and for the Michigan win. We will remember we were privileged to witness the beginning of their lives together, and, of course, a joyous Michigan win.

Lest you think I have forgotten that this is a legal newspaper and that I imagine I am writing for some bride's magazine, I will remind you that I was witness to the sealing of a contract; the man offered, she accepted, and there was consideration in the form of a ring.

Also, it was rumored that U.S. Supreme Court Chief Justice Roberts was at the game. I didn't see him. And I am quite sure there were a few lawyers in the crowd; however, I suspect that is enough law for one sunny, exciting, joyful, September football Saturday afternoon.

On Chicken Coops and the Law

For reasons unknown, I decided that I wanted to raise some chickens on my writer- daughter's small farm (aka Rockin L Ranch) located in mid-Michigan. The first step was to ask her if I could do this. She said, "Sure, supply the food and shelter."

Great! But first, some serious research was in order. So off I went to the County Extension office, the Internet and the local library. County Extension supplied me with several booklets and pamphlets on different types of chickens, the care of chickens, the breeding of chickens, the showing of chickens and the housing of chickens. Ah, yes, housing. We needed a chicken coop.

The Internet supplied information on housing chickens. A chicken coop could be ordered from England but the cost was prohibitive, what with the exchange rate and the shipping.

Building plans were available from various agricultural schools. There were personal anecdotal accounts of building chicken coops. The information collected revealed that chicken coops should face south for light and air. Their shape—lower on the south edge, higher on the north edge, is designed to retain heat in cold climates and to be tall enough for a human to stand up in to clean.

We decided to buy a pre-cut shed and adapt it. But first we had to clear a spot in the field.

We picked a day of low winds declared by the fire department to be okay for setting fires. We set the field on fire. All was well until we realized we had no permit and the fire appeared to be getting out of hand.

After the firemen left, we had a nice spot of ground adequately cleared. The volunteer firemen were quite pleased to be called out. They had to suit up, put out the fire and clean all the equipment, an all-day task calling for comradery and time away from home duties.

Now to select the coop. We were off to Home Depot to look. To construct a coop from plans would call for purchasing lumber, reading and following blueprints, cutting everything. A feat way beyond our capabilities. We selected a nice garden shed. It was approximately the desired shape, had four skylights, a window for light, a window box and an adorable Dutch door. It was most satisfactory. It was ordered. Three weeks later, a tall stack of flat boxes and much lumber, not in the shape of a chicken coop at all, arrived.

In the meantime, we needed to select the spot. Remember, our research dictated that it must face south. Going to the cleared field, the grandsons (aged nine and five) and I stood with our arms spread wide to approximate the size of the coop in the field. Writer-daughter had us move around until the perfect spot was found.

Finally, we set to work. This should not be too difficult. We have the directions. We have our garden aprons securely tied around our waists. Tools are in place, hats on. We are ready. The directions. Hmmm. The directions. Between the two of us we have five college degrees. We can write and reason. The problem? This does not call for reason. We cannot intuit this shed to completion. We have to follow the directions. Following directions is totally foreign but, follow directions, we must.

Working weekends over the course of the summer, progress on the coop was slow. Many times we had to carry pieces to the job site and hold them in place in order to figure out what to do. The trusses for the roof were very difficult. They were triangles, for goodness sake. We hung the Dutch door upside down, easily corrected when called to our attention by my helpful son-in- law who generally and wisely left us to our own devices.

In spite of our lack of experience, the work moved forward without major incident. The attorney member of the team set her garden apron to smoldering by placing two charged batteries and one metal knife in the same pocket. Upon smelling the fire, we discussed who was burning that day and other possible sources of the smell before realizing that I was smoking. Taking off the apron solved the problem. The fire was stamped out leaving a small hole.

On the batteries, it says: "Do not store or carry battery so that metal objects can contact metal edge. Short circuit could cause fire or burns or damage to battery." Who knew?

(Attorney-builder also has a huge ink stain on her garden apron from placing an uncapped felt tip marker in the pocket. Writer-daughter's apron is pristine.)

Why do We do That?

What does all this have to do with the law? A great deal. The entire project was subject to one law or another. The purchase of the shed was covered by the UCC. The window had to be returned due to damage in shipping—it was covered by the warranty. Township ordinances required a fire permit for our own protection.

Government regulations help, but only because attorneys file lawsuits to make parties obey the rules. The battery incident could have been avoided had attorney-builder bothered to read the warning label on the battery, undoubtedly there as a result of a court case at one time. Flame-retardant material required in the construction of the apron prevented it from bursting into flames. Much maligned trial attorneys have protected us from unscrupulous manufacturers.

When we hear all the attorney jokes and we begin to believe our own bad press, remember the chicken coop and the laws involved which quietly assisted two untrained but eager builders to joyfully build in relative safety.

Why do We do That?

The Law and...

Everywhere we turn we run into the law. As I write this, it is Valentine's Day. It has snowed and is still snowing. When you read this, it should be the end of March and perhaps, warm. Ah, Spring. But I digress, back to the law.

Law and Valentine's Day. Not a real holiday at all, it's a day to send cards and flowers and candy. A day for interstate commerce, the Internet and copyright. A day of infamy—the St. Valentine's day massacre—which calls into play criminal law.

Law and snow. The law did not create snow; but let that beautiful stuff get on the ground and it becomes a subject of the law. If more than two inches falls on the sidewalk, it shall be shoveled. Mail will only be delivered if the route to the mailbox is cleared. So, we shovel the snow. The shovel is subject to its own laws.

Law and the family dog. Promise, a dog of much patience, likes to help shovel the snow. She does this by leaping and biting at the snow as it flies off the shovel and through the air. She does not like to be on her leash while she helps with the snow. The law says she must be attached to a human in some way. Our answer is to shovel early, before we can be observed. We use an invisible leash. This method, a small technical violation, has worked very well.

Law and the cat. No law there. Grizzabella sits in the window, paws tucked. She watches with disdain and amusement as the human throws snow and the dog leaps and bites. Sitting up, she washes an invisible dust mote off her face. She thinks her own thoughts and follows her own rules. Human laws have no meaning for her.

Law and food. It is time for breakfast. A long look in the refrigerator reveals the effects of many laws. The food comes with a date. The date tells us when the food is bad and should not be eaten. In the past, if the food smelled strange or bore a strong resemblance to a science experiment, one knew not to eat it. Now we are told. Evidently we needed that information.

Why do We do That?

More law and food. The labels on the food tell us much more than we wish to know.

Mercy, look at the fat content. So much sugar. Way too much salt. Is there enough fiber? Is five a lot or a little? What am I suppose to avoid? What to include? Breakfast has become a minefield of choices and at least one of which will be wrong, thanks to the law.

Law and morning ablutions. There is nothing simple here. Bathroom products are covered with facts and warnings. "Do not eat." "Do not apply to broken skin." "Do not use in combination with topical products." Do not, do not, DO NOT. Working carefully and swiftly, the bathroom is conquered. Relieved to be done with the potential legal entanglements, we move on to the closet.

Law and the fashion business. It is hard to say what laws the fashion mavens follow. There are the laws of interstate commerce. Those laws are handy but not terribly important to designers. Most designers prefer having their names displayed prominently on your person for all to see. We in Ann Arbor are not strongly influenced by fashion. An Oakland County attorney told me that we were a little rumpled. Imagine that! We do know the law, however, even if the fashion mavens don't.

Law and the briefcase. Now it is time to leave the house. Into the briefcase goes the cellular phone. (Why is it called cellular? I shall have to inquire of the engineer types to find the answer to that question.) At any rate, it and the laws surrounding it go into the briefcase. Next, the Day Timer, or for the more technologically advanced, the Palm Pilot. Must be some law there. Perhaps one of the files in the briefcase might have some law in its murky depths. We wouldn't know since it never left the briefcase in spite of our good intentions when we brought it home.

Law and the car. To keep the gendarmes from your door, all snow must be scraped off the car so your view of other drivers is unobstructed. You must drive carefully and observe the rules of common sense to avoid striking another car. Using hand gestures to show your concern for the driving of others is disfavored and could lead to conflict with the law. So, we hop into the car, drive down the freshly shoveled driveway, and onto the not-so-freshly plowed street. Now we are completely covered by law.

Why do We do That?

Law and the lawyer. Laws are our business: helpful laws, confusing or confining laws, annoying laws, laws for all seasons and occasions and laws for all people. There are laws with which we agree and laws with which we disagree. Daily, we work with them all and, to our amusement and sometimes amazement, we do our work well.

Why do We do That?

Dumb Laws, Wise Laws

The Internet, where it is possible to find almost anything, is the spot to squander many hours going from one link to another to find useful or useless information. Whether that capability is good, bad or indifferent is open to debate. The bottom line is that someone has put something on the Net for you to read. A website of interest to lawyers wishing to spend rather amusing unbillable time is called dumblaws.com.

The site is organized in such a way that one can find what the authors determine to be the dumb laws from almost any state in the Union as well as from many countries. The site planners take contributions in the form of other dumb laws from those of us who peruse their site. Topics include not only laws from around the world but also dumb criminals, dumb warnings or dumb facts.

Grand Haven, MI: No person shall throw an abandoned hoop skirt into any street or on any sidewalk, under penalty of a five dollar fine for each offense.

Imagine, if you will, that you are riding your horse down the main street of Grand Haven. The wind is in your hair, you can see beautiful Lake Michigan, the sun is rising on a beautiful spring day, and all is right with the world. Suddenly, your horse rears, startled by something in the road. You struggle and manage to stay on the bucking horse. Looking down, what do you see? What is the cause of the horse's fear? An abandoned hoop skirt, left on the street by revelers from the previous night. Not such a dumb law, after all.

Many of the laws had to do with our interaction with animals—both wild and domestic. It is illegal to tie your alligator to a fire hydrant in Detroit. The city of Ludington is exempted from the state law prohibiting the running of cattle, hogs or sheep through the streets of towns of over 7,000 folks. This exemption is possibly because of its status as a port city. In the city of Wayland, anyone can keep a cow on Main Street at a cost of 3 cents a day. In Clawson, it is legal for a farmer to sleep with his pigs, cows, horses, goats or chickens. Why he would want to do so is unclear.

Why do We do That?

In the state of Michigan there is a ten-cent bounty for each rat's head brought into the town office. There is also a ten-cent bounty for each crow, a three-cent bounty for each starling and two-cent bounty for each English sparrow.

One can understand the bounty on rats, what with the plague and all. In days past when the government was much smaller, there was no trash collection, hence the need to control the rats. But, why the bounty on the birds?

In 1890 about 100 starlings, non-native birds about eight inches long, were released in New York's Central Park. By 1940, the birds had arrived in California. They travel in large flocks, foraging and damaging orchards and feedlots of domestic cattle in their quest for food. They were, and I suspect still are, a nuisance to the community. Hence, there is a bounty to encourage their demise and a purpose for the law.

The Crows: The common crow in Michigan and other states is a large black bird (about 17 to 21 inches in length) that likes city and country life. They seem to like University life also.

Being social beings, as many as two or three hundred will roost together in the trees. They warn each other and other animals of approaching danger. The crow eats our garbage as well as seeds, mice and insects. In Japan, the crows dive-bomb the citizens strolling in the park. They steal coat hangers to use in building nests. A versatile bird, much maligned in the past. Not so now, but the law is still on the books.

The English sparrow was brought from England and introduced to Central Park in 1850. Twenty years later, it had reached California. By 1940, it could be found all over the United States. As hard as the law and the bounty hunters tried, they could not stop its progression. It now ranges from Alaska to southernmost South America.

The law tries its best to control human behavior. The purposes of the laws, however, change with the times.

Kalamazoo: It is against the law to serenade your girlfriend. While it may be legal to serenade the members of the family or your friends, you may not sing with romance in your heart.

Rochester: All bathing suits must be inspected by the head of the Police. So on the first Monday of every month, after an exciting weekend of shopping, the citizens of Rochester can present their bathing suits for examination. Such inspections may have been required in the interests of human decency as determined by the customs or the costumes of the day.

Detroit: A person may not willfully destroy his or her radio. This law was probably enacted when radio was the only means of communicating with the citizens of Detroit. In the interests of preserving families, the husbands of Detroit may not scowl at their wives on Sunday. Not even when she interrupts the football game of the day as the time is running out and the receiver is about to catch the winning touchdown. Not even then.

The laws on dumblaws.com appear dumb on the surface. If, however, we view them in light of the customs of the times in which the good citizens of the community enacted them, they are not so dumb after all. In some cases, they may even have seemed wise. At least that's a thought.

Why do We do That?

Y2K? The Law Is Ready

"One of the most potentially devastating events this nation has ever encountered." (US Senate Y2K report) "If today were January 1, 2000, the world's airline system would fail." (same report, pg. 71) Predictions abound. Standing in line at the grocery store has become increasingly alarming. One is bombarded with, "More than 30 million people in the United States are likely to be without water after January 2000." Or, "Severe long- and short-term disruptions to supply chains are likely to occur."

What is causing all this concern? Two facts: 1) the world has become increasingly dependent on computers; and 2) at one time numerous computer programmers, in an effort to save space and without thinking about future dates, used only two digits rather than four to indicate the year. Therefore, many systems read the date 2000 as 1900.

Computers, it is believed, will be confused and unable to function. So, one tiny little shortcut will create one big mess.

If that "mess" does occur (or if you are reading this after January 1 of 2000 and it did occur) it could be that you will be reading by candlelight. Will society come to a grinding halt? Some areas of society may, but (dum-de-dum-dum) the law will not. We are prepared. We can adapt to a simpler society.

Well, the majority of us can. Those who remember books—actual volumes with hard covers and paper upon which words are printed—are ready. We know how to use card catalogues or encyclopedias to find those words. Assuming some wise librarian kept the card catalogue, we can look up "law stuff." We remember the stacks of books in the dark recesses of the library. We can find our way among all those dusty, long-forgotten books to the exact cases we need.

And what will we find? We will find that because the law has developed over time through judges' decisions piling up one upon the other, we can go back to simpler times. The doctrine of precedent is a two-way street. We can drive in either direction.

Why do We do That?

If one should find animals running at large because electric fences no longer work, the case of Elisha Cook vs Harrison W. Bossett, Washtenaw Circuit, September 1870, will solve any disputes. Mr. Bossett found a cow walking down the highway in front of his house. The cow was alone. He put the cow in his barn and notified the magistrate. Elisha came to get his cow and was told it would cost him 50 cents. Elisha decided to sue for the return of his cow.

However, the law of 1867 provided that found animals could be sold at auction after proper notice of seizure was posted. Both auctioneer and seizer could collect expenses from the proceeds. Thus, should you find a cow, simply follow the procedure as outlined in Cook, and your problem is solved.

Thinking of taking up fishing to provide fresh fish for dinner? Try stake fishing with nets. The justices in the 1884 case of Lincoln v Davis granted those owning land along the Michigan lakes exclusive fishing with stationary nets for one mile from low-water mark, But, warned the court, beyond that limit one has no right, as riparian owner merely, to interfere with stake-fishing by others.

No matter what you drive, be it horse and buggy or your car (assuming it has no computer and still works), you cannot drive negligently. The law of homicide through the negligent driving goes back to English common law.

Consider the case of Rex v Timmins, (1836). The defendant was charged with driving an omnibus so negligently that it overturned and killed the deceased. "The question here is, whether the prisoner was driving in such a negligent manner that he lost command of his horses. for a man is not to say, I will race along a road, and when I am got past another carriage, I will pull up. If the prisoner did really race, and only when he had got past another omnibus endeavored to pull up, he must be found guilty."

In Hale's Pleas of the Crown (first published in 1716), it is said, "it is the duty of any man who drives any carriage, to drive it with such care and caution as to prevent, as far as in his power, any accident or injury that may occur." Use care and caution as you go along and all will be well.

House has no water or heat? The solution may be to go live with a relative who has these amenities in the form of a well, a fireplace, and wood stove. Should you find that life-style to your liking you could make an agreement similar to one made by Diana and John Thompson. They agreed to support Diana's father during his lifetime in exchange for the conveyance of the father's lands to her upon his death. But after the father's death, the other relatives complained. The Court, in the 1870 case of Goff v Thompson, held for Diana, saying that the consideration for the deed was good and sufficient; the condition having been performed, there could be no doubt that the title of the defendants, John and Diana, to the land was good.

The Court added, "The conduct of the defendants, John and Diana Thompson, seems to have been not only just, but meritorious." Make your agreement, move in and enjoy your new life knowing that your interests are protected.

As you can see, the Law will be ready. While others are storing water, food and other essentials, and wondering how they will survive without the Internet, lawyers can rest easy knowing that there are solutions for any problems their clients may face. Whether by candlelight or electric light, a little research will reveal a most satisfactory answer.

Why do We do That?

My Summer Vacation or The FBI vs. The ATF

Writer-daughter (hereinafter identified as MP (multi-published) writer-daughter, having sold four books to electronic publishers this year) and I spent some time in Washington, DC, for the annual Romance Writer's Convention. The Romantic-Suspense section of the group—appropriately named the Kiss of Death—arranged for its members to tour the FBI and the ATF. The purpose of the tours for the writers was to learn investigative techniques and possibly see examples of attractive men for heroes of their books. The purpose of the tour for the FBI was and still is unclear. The purpose for the ATF tour was to explain to us what they do.

The trip began in the hotel lobby where the thirty or so of us drank coffee, ate bagels, chatted, read the paper and waited. First we waited for the bus to arrive. Unlike the airlines, it was on time. Then we had to wait to be summoned by the FBI. Some time passed. Finally, we were told to board the bus for the trip. The driver was very knowledgeable about the sights along the way.

As we approached the FBI building, the driver warned us in no uncertain terms that we would not be able to take anything into the FBI. This is the Federal Bureau of Investigation, we are told. This is serious business. We must be alert. We must not create any suspicion. If we do, we will not be allowed into the facility or, worse yet, not allowed to leave. We are required to go through security. From his tone, we know the FBI is adamant about security.

We pulled up to the building labeled Federal Bureau of Investigation. It is a gray cement flattish government building with a wide dry moat encircling it. One could easily imagine the moat flooded with water, drawbridge drawn up for safety. Timidly, we disembarked and stood in line to enter the building. Most of us walked through with nothing in our hands. Those brave enough to bring a fanny pack place it on the conveyer belt. We walk through the scanner.

Success, we were all admitted.

Why do We do That?

Herding us into a reasonably large, dimly lit, low-ceilinged room, we were given coloring books describing the FBI.

"Are these materials appropriate for our reading level?" I asked writer-daughter.

"I guess they think so," she answered.

Scanning the coloring books was instructive. In five pages the steps between investigation, arrest and the resultant conviction were clearly shown. There was no mention of rights, no mention of presumption of innocence, and, strangely, no mention of a defense attorney. The reader was led to believe that arrest automatically leads to conviction. This could be a reasonable conclusion from a group that wears only navy blue and talks into the lapel of its jacket.

The tour began with an explanation of the "CODIS" system by special agent Jennifer Smith of the DNA unit. "CODIS" stands for Combined DNA Index System maintained by the FBI and similar to the fingerprinting database.

"Regretfully," said agent Smith, "not all states cooperate with the system."

I leave you to your own thoughts on that point. After her discussion, we are divided into groups of five led by women tour guides. Where are the "hunky" men? Warning us not to stray, we are led through the facility.

We see the laboratory with boxes of evidence sitting around as if in a mailroom and people in white lab coats looking intense and performing tests. We see a vacuum room with a large table on which an exhibit is placed to be vacuumed for trace evidence. Some of the ceiling tiles in this sterile room are hanging down. One wonders about the little mouse that drops down from the ceiling, runs over the evidence leaving behind his little mouse hairs all the while laughing at the confusion he creates. Let us hope he knows a good defense attorney.

The finale of this tour was a visit to the target range where a man—the first we had seen— demonstrates his shooting prowess. He shoots a pistol and a rifle and makes lots of noise. We all clap. He explains that all of the 12,000 agents currently employed by the FBI have to qualify with various weapons. It must be a fact that they qualify as only 34 agents have been killed in the line of duty or as a result of a training accident. Apparently, the job of FBI agent is a very safe job.

Why do We do That?

After being led through the gift shop, yes, Virginia, they have a gift shop, we are back on the bus and off to the Bureau of Alcohol, Tobacco and Firearms that trains at the DC Police Academy. The ATF men and women welcomed us with no security and lots of information. We were given cool baseball caps the ATF logo and Explosives K-9 embroidered on the crown. This writer and others of my generation immediately put on the caps as the sun was bright. The younger members of the group did not.

We entered a large gym at the facility where the writers of the group listened to the briefing, while looking around at the men in the ATF, as well as those in the weight room overlooking the gym, for hero material for their next book. ATF agents are experts in explosives and arson. They are trained to investigate and determine the type of bomb used. They detonate or diffuse bombs and investigate arson.

After a discussion by a profiler, we divided into groups. We moved outdoors to five different workstations. We saw bomb suits, a large trailer housing a lab, an investigation vehicle and   a K-9 unit. We met a real fire investigator. A yellow lab named Cascade, a member of the K- 9 unit, showed us how she could locate explosive material. Her workstation was very popular.

The fire investigator gave each of us an interactive virtual reality fire investigation CD for our computer. No coloring books here, just hard facts, open air and lots of information. Also there was no gift shop.

At the end of the day, the writers knew a great deal about the ATF, had an impression of the FBI, and had material for new plots and new characters. The creative minds of the writers will use some or all that was seen on that day. One wonders what the ATF or the FBI will do with what they observed.

Why do We do That?

The Pet Who Broke The Rules

As some of you know, I have pets. Promise, the dog of much patience. Grizzabella, the cat of great dignity and little brain. The pets are subject to certain rules of the household. Grizz is there to protect the homeowner from attack by small, furry creatures that belong outside. (This homeowner does not fear death or taxes but does view mice, snakes and possibly some judges with alarm.) Promise is there to force said homeowner to take daily walks in an effort to forestall infirmity. Those are the rules.

One evening recently, the homeowner, AKA "lady lawyer," is busy on the Net researching important legal stuff. Promise, an Australian Shepherd bred for herding, is normally quick on her paws. She is, however, done for the day and sleeping peacefully. Grizz is nowhere to be seen. A fire burns in the fireplace. All is right with the world.

Suddenly, Grizz races down the hall, an amazing feat for a cat of advanced years. Promise leaps up and joins the chase. Of what, one wonders? Checking on this amazing burst of energy, a mouse is seen. It is huge being at least two inches long with an inch and a half tail. It dashes for the living room with the pets in hot pursuit.

Grizz is a politically correct cat; she will only catch and release. And she is not doing a good job of that. Promise stands with legs planted firmly, ears pricked, and watches the scene, only showing some concern when mouse and Grizz run under her belly.

Homeowner throws a towel over the mouse, which does nothing but confuse the cat. The broom, which could be used to sweep the creature outside, seems to have disappeared. The cat is not following the rules. There is only one solution: grab the mouse by its tail and put it outside. It is a well-known fact that mice will run up your leg, so this solution must be approached with caution. After several attempts, it is accomplished. The mouse is captured and deposited outside to tell his mouse friends that here is a safe house with a useless cat. The "For Let" sign is out.

Why do We do That?

Litigation is in order. Homeowner files a complaint seeking damages for intentional infliction of emotional distress, breach of contract, breaking of the rules, and other allegations too numerous to mention. Grizz answers. We are in locked battle.

But, maybe not. Alternative Dispute Resolution (ADR), defined as any process designed to resolve a legal dispute in place of court adjudication, is available. If deemed appropriate after consulting with the parties, a court can submit a case to an appropriate ADR process.

What are those processes? A settlement conference, a setting familiar to legal folk, case evaluation—formerly know as mediation and, again, familiar and mediation—a process where a neutral third party facilitates communication between the parties, assists in identifying issues, and helps explore solutions to reach a mutually acceptable settlement. Mediators have no authoritative decision-making powers—they merely help the parties reach a solution.

Homeowner and Grizz decide to try mediation.

Who will mediate this dispute? If homeowner and Grizz can agree on a mediator from the court list of approved mediators or on someone from the community and not on the list, then the court will accept that individual. If we can't agree, the court can appoint a mediator from its own list. We select Promise, the dog of much patience, to mediate the dispute even though she has not had the requisite training.

What training? Completion of a training program approved by the State Court Administrator, a JD degree or a degree in conflict resolution, 40 hours of mediation experience, observation of general mediation proceedings and advanced training every two years. Promise has none of this but as we agree on her as mediator, she can perform that function.

What fees will she charge? She merely asks for a special dog bone of which she is very fond. Other mediators might want cash based on an hourly rate commensurate with their experience and usual charges for the services performed. The cost of the dog bone is divided equally between homeowner and Grizz.

How is the mediation conducted? We meet in Promise's favorite spot, the kitchen. She listens carefully to each of us, determining the facts and issues of the matter. She knows homeowner wants her house free of small, furry animals. She hears Grizz say she has a problem with killing and prefers catch and release, to be caught and released another day.

Why do We do That?

After much discussion, a settlement is reached. Homeowner will purchase several mousetraps to catch any unwelcome guests. Grizz will notify homeowner of the presence of the visitors so that traps can be set. Within seven days, Promise notifies the court that the mediation has been successful. The necessary documents needed to conclude the case are filed with the court within twenty-one days. The matter is resolved.

Peace has been restored without lengthy litigation. Grizzabella rests during the day to be ready for duty at night. Promise is pleased with her bone. Homeowner has purchased the traps to be ready for the mice that see and believe the "For Let" sign left in the yard.

It was a most satisfactory and speedy dispute resolution. ADR is here to stay. It may be the answer for over-crowded dockets and for both attorneys and litigants frustrated with a cumbersome legal process that often leaves both sides dissatisfied. Time will tell.